LC
5219
.043
1995

Non-Credit Instruction:
A Guide for Continuing and Adult Education Programs

Lea Leever Oldham

INFO-TEC, Inc. ♦ Cleveland, Ohio

DAVID L. RICE LIBRARY
UNIVERSITY OF SOUTHERN INDIANA
EVANSVILLE, IN

Order information:

INFO-TEC, Inc.
P.O. Box 40092
Cleveland, Ohio 44140
(216) 333-3157
FAX (216) 933-9285
© 1995, by Info-Tec, Inc.
ISBN 0-940017-20-2

All rights reserved. No part of this publication may be reproduced, stored in a retrieval system, or transmitted, in any form or by any means, electronic, mechanical, photocopying, recording, or otherwise, without the prior written permission of the copyright owner.

Printed in the United States of America

Forward

It is said that a renowned educator, early in the progressive education movement, once stated "the first steps in learning is confusion." If so, that can aptly be applied to the role of teaching, especially to those of you who have elected to teach in non-traditional situations such as non-credit classes, seminar instruction and classes containing students with differing ages and backgrounds.

This publication, ***Non-Credit Instruction: A Guide for Continuing and Adult Education Programs,*** is designed to help instructors through the initial "confusing" elements of preparing for and presenting non-credit classes. Non-credit education, instruction without the threat or motivation of grades, can be the most rewarding of all teaching experiences. It is not, however, easier or less important than credit instruction, and the responsibility and role of the instructor may be more important and demanding than the role of traditional instruction.

This publication, intended for both beginning and experienced teachers, provides an introspective look at students and their concerns, the role of the teacher, techniques for successful instruction, as well as actual support documents for effective non-credit instruction. It is intended to provide a resource to assist you to experience success in your non-credit teaching endeavors.

Donald Greive, Ed.D.
Editor

ABOUT THE AUTHOR

Lea Leever Oldham has been teaching non-credit classes for over twenty years at Lakeland Community College in Kirtland, Ohio, and other educational institutions. She was Small Business Management Instructor for the Ohio Department of Education for three and a half years and continues to teach small business, writing, and human resource development subjects throughout northeastern Ohio.

She is coordinator of the Western Reserve Writers and Freelance Conference which she founded in 1983. She is owner of Images to Impress, a management consulting firm specializing in training employees of business, government, and nonprofit organizations. Her articles have been published in *The Writer, New Woman, The Living Church, American Nurseryman, Woman, Entrepreneur, Aquaculture, Ohio Magazine,* and many other national, regional, and trade magazines.

CONTENTS

Techniques for Teaching Non-credit Classes 6
Introduction
    What is Continuing Education? 6
The Class
    What's the Difference Between Credit
        and Non-credit Classes? 6
    Planning and Presenting Your Class 8
    Naming the Course and Writing the Description 8
    Marketing the Course 10
        Sample Press Releases 11
    Other Ways to Promote Your Class 13
    Planning the Class 13
        Sample Course Outline 15
The Instruction
    Who Teaches Non-credit Classes? 17
    The First Class 17
    Classroom Techniques 20
The Students
    Who Takes Your Classes? 23
    Student Behaviors & Teaching Techniques 24
    Considerations When Teaching Older Adults 27
Evaluation
    What if They Don't Come Back? 28
    How Do You Know if They Learned Anything? 28
    Teacher's Self-evaluation 30

Techniques for Teaching Non-credit Classes

"To educate you must inform and entertain," is probably a paraphrase of Plato's, "Let education of the young be a form of amusement." This doesn't mean a teacher should be a stand-up comic, but instructors are expected to make the subject interesting enough to keep the students' interest. Nowhere is this truer than in non-credit classes and continuing education.

Introduction

What is Continuing Education?

As more of us come to realize our learning didn't end when we earned our last diploma or degree, we seek out places where we can continue our learning in subjects ranging from professional education to personal skill development. Continuing Education is offered by colleges and universities, public school districts, community entities, and local governments. Non-credit courses and seminars are designed to meet the lifelong learning needs of local residents. The classes are directed at all age groups, from young people to retirees.

In the mid-eighties, Tom Applegate, head of Ohio's Adult Education, stated that "The number of Adult Education students in the state's public school systems exceeded all students in secondary education." He added that he saw no end to this rising trend. Today, the continual expansion of programs within educational institutions; the addition of programs in colleges and other providers of education where non-credit courses were not offered a few years ago; and the rising development of for-profit firms offering programs, attest to how on-target his predictions were.

The Class

What's the Difference Between Credit and Non-credit

There are differences between credit and non-credit classes. Students in primary, secondary, and higher education <u>must</u> attend classes, because the law requires it, parents insist, credentials need to be acquired, or all of the above.

Students in non-credit classes do not have to attend classes. This doesn't mean students in non-credit courses are less committed than in credit classes. They may be more committed in attendance and attention because they really want the information they can acquire to help them in their career, their personal lives, or in other interests. Students may have enrolled in classes in Total Quality Management, Customer Service, Sales, or any of hundreds of specialized and technical classes to help them advance in their professions. Many will be reimbursed by their employers at the end of course. If they're not, they at least know the information will help them advance in their occupation or to enrich their personal lives. As a result, non-credit students may be more committed to learning than some students in credit classes who may not yet have learned the value of education.

The hundreds of non-credit subjects offered by various educational institutions, school districts, and government entities are structured in many different ways. Some courses last a full semester, although no grade is given at the end of the course. Even though students are not graded, certificates may be offered since more professions require CEUs for certification or renewal. At the other end of the spectrum are one-day or one-night workshops or seminars for subjects not requiring as many hours of class time. Between these two extremes are seminars or workshops lasting more than one day or night, but less than a full semester. Length is determined by the topic and the needs of the students.

As an instructor, you should keep track of attendance, particularly if CEUs are given. Also be aware of students who may leave the classroom on a break and not return, or those who simply don't come back for the next session. When these situations occur, it's possible the student is sick, bored, or needed at home. Even the most experienced and capable non-credit teacher has students disappear occasionally. You have no control over students becoming ill or having personal reasons for not attending classes. But you have the responsibility to be prepared, to watch for signs of boredom, and to involve your students in the class so you'll know their needs.

Planning and Presenting the Class

If your course appeals to people who work outside the home, allow enough time for them to get home from work, eat, and get to class. A six o'clock starting time might cut down registration while a seven o'clock class might be more attractive. After you teach a class for a semester or two, you may wish to change the starting time or increase or decrease the number of hours the class is held. You may also find students want additional information on a specific subject. In the future you may want to teach an advanced version of a class. Often you don't know how a class is going to work until you've taught it.

After you've estimated how many hours you'll need for the class, decide on the length of each session. Let's say you feel you can cover the subject in twelve hours. Should you have six two-hour classes, four three-hour classes, or two six-hour classes? Would you use a hands-on approach? More than a few teachers have offered a class one way then changed the scheduling as they learned what worked best. If you plan to teach computer programming, cooking, or wallpapering, you need equipment and facilities where hands-on classes can be offered. When scheduling for specific equipment and/or facilities, the Continuing Education department makes the final decision on dates, times, and places.

Naming the Course and Writing the Description

When you've established your qualifications to teach a subject and provided an outline, you have to put a title on it, write a description, along with the time and length of the class. Some subjects lend themselves to "cute" titles more than others. But if you opt for a clever title, make sure it clearly describes the subject you're teaching. Otherwise, you could either end up with a witty title but no students or with students who took the class thinking it was something it wasn't. (The latter can happen even with the most descriptive title.)

One teacher offered a class entitled "How to Self-publish Your Own Book," which seemed specific enough. The course included deciding whether a particular topic lent itself to self-publishing and what steps were required if self-publishing was the choice. The teacher had offered it at least a dozen times without problems. But one night, after questioning the students for this one-night class, she found all seven signed up thinking they'd learn how to sell their books to publishers. Despite the course description, it was misunderstood by this group.

You might find renaming an existing class increases enrollment. When "Communication Between the Sexes," was changed to "Did You Marry an Alien?" Registration doubled and remained high. When doing this, make sure to include "Formerly . . ." the first few times so students don't accidentally sign up for a class they've already taken. When "How to Operate Your Own Small Business" was retitled "B.Y.O.B. (Build Your Own Business)" enrollment also increased and remained high. Originally, this was to stand for Be Your Own Boss but worked better as Build Your Own Business since it attracted people who not only wanted to start their own small business, but also those in business.

When writing the description for the course, keep in mind the benefit to the student. A potential student could be attracted to an antique class by the statement "Learn how to separate real antiques from reproductions. Discover the best places to look for bargains." Think about why a person would take your class and what would appeal to him or her.

Find out the deadline for turning in your descriptions and dates. If students are to bring specific equipment to class, either include this information in the description and/or contact enrolled students by phone or mail to alert them of requirements. Don't try to cover everything in one class. For instance, instead of including all aspects of job hunting strategies in one class, it might be preferable to offer one series on resume writing and cover letters; another on interviewing skills; and another on tapping the hidden job market. Doing it this way offers students the opportunity to take the sections they feel they need help in without sitting through information they may already have. When teaching sequential subjects, and offering them individually, suggest the institution offer a special price for taking the whole series. Some institutions have set prices and others are willing to discuss fees with teachers. If you feel the fee is too high or too low, express your opinion. But be aware, institutions make their own rules and you have the option of following them or teaching elsewhere.

Marketing the Course

Promoting your courses will improve enrollment as well as endear you to the those in charge of the sponsoring group.

If you're teaching several courses, hand out a list of upcoming classes to your students. When students get to know and like you, they'll come back for more of your classes and recommend them to co-workers, family members, and friends.

Some continuing or adult education departments send out press releases. Whether yours does or not, you can send out your own to promote your classes. Before sending out releases, check with those in charge so they know your plans. Send one for each course instead of trying to consolidate them all on one release. Get the important facts in the first paragraph, answering those age-old questions, What, Where, Why, Who, and How. Then expand on the first paragraph in succeeding paragraphs. Editors cut from the bottom up when space is limited; this way you'll have the important information included.

Determine where to send each release. If your course is business-related, send it to the business editor of a daily paper. If it involves women's issues, send it to the editor of that section; many dailies call that the Living section. If your courses might appeal to physically-active men and women, direct your release to the sports editor. If your paper includes a calendar of upcoming events, send the basics to that section also. Press releases to daily and weekly newspapers should be sent out about three weeks in advance of when you want them to appear.

Don't overlook special publications in your area which target women, small business, seniors, business and industry, minority groups, culture, and other segments of the society. For monthly publications, send releases at least two months in advance. If you have free shopper type papers in your area, send releases to them three weeks in advance. People read many of these shoppers more thoroughly than daily papers.

Remember organization newsletters such as those published by Chambers of Commerce, women's groups, small business organizations, senior centers, communities, religious groups, and trade organizations. Send these out at least two months in advance. Local libraries often have listings of organizations. Watch your newspaper for information about new clubs and organizations. Trade organizations are usually listed in the Yellow Pages of your phone book. Trade organizations may even be interested in co-sponsoring a course. If you can work this out, the organization will promote it and your course will have increased credibility.

For general listings of media in your community, visit the library for media directories or call your local Press Organization or Club or Public Relations Society of America branches. Many of these chapters have updated media directories and may be willing to send you one.

Press releases for the print media are not dated but are sent with the contact name, address, and phone number at the top. Printed stationery is ideal for this. The opening line is **"FOR IMMEDIATE RELEASE."** Indent paragraphs and double space the entire release. Try to get everything on one page. If you can't, type "MORE" at the bottom of the first page and continue on second page. At the end of the release type **"THE END,"** and do not staple. If you keep the release to one page, it has a better chance of getting picked up. Press releases can also lead to feature articles when editors and/or reporters contact you for additional information.

Radio and TV spots should contain only the barest essentials and be headed **"PUBLIC SERVICE ANNOUNCEMENT"** at the top. Also include time required to read. Count the words in the announcement and divide by 25, then multiply by 10 to get the number of seconds needed. In other words a 75-word announcement takes 30 seconds to read. You'll have your best chance of getting your announcement on the air if it reaches the station at least four weeks in advance.

Sample Press Release for Print Media

Use letterhead or write:
Contact: Name
Phone number:

FOR IMMEDIATE RELEASE

Men and women who dream of owning their own business can learn how at a seminar on Saturday, November 5, at Lakeland Community College, Kirtland, from 9 a.m. to 4 p.m. The seminar, BYOB (Build Your Own Business) covers available resources; legal considerations, sole proprietorships, partnerships, and corporations; and CPA Joan Baizel speaking about deductions, bookkeeping basics, and the ever-changing tax laws.

Other subjects to be covered include marketing strategy and other basics. Business owner and former Small Business Management Instructor for the Ohio Department of Education Lea Leever Oldham leads the seminar. Participants can eat in Lakeland's cafeteria or local restaurants during the one-hour lunch break.

For further information, call Lakeland Lifelong Learning, 953-7116. Registration is $39 can be made by phone using MasterCard or Visa. Checks may be sent to Lakeland Lifelong Learning, 7700 Clocktower Dr., Kirtland, OH 44094.

THE END

Sample Press Release for Radio and Television

Use letterhead or write:
Contact: Name
Phone number:
30 Seconds

PUBLIC SERVICE ANNOUNCEMENT

BYOB stands for Build Your Own Business and is the title of a seminar to be held on Saturday, November 5, at Lakeland Community College, Kirtland, from 9 a.m. to 4 p.m.

For further information, call Lakeland Lifelong Learning, 953-7116. Registration is $39 can be made by phone using MasterCard or Visa. Checks may be sent to Lakeland Lifelong Learning, 7700 Clocktower Dr., Kirtland, OH 44094.

THE END

Other Ways to Promote Your Classes

Think about other ways to reach people who might be interested in your classes. Libraries are usually willing to display handouts promoting educational opportunities. Design a one-page flyer and print it on a brightly colored paper which will attract attention. Just make sure it isn't a dark color which is hard to read. If your course would appeal to seniors, drop off flyers at senior centers. If you're teaching a course for business and there is a business conference or after-hours get-together, take your flyers to that event. If it's a craft-related topic, take flyers to local craft shows. The possibilities are unlimited, keep your eyes open for new and different ways to market your course. Some McDonald's restaurants even print monthly placemats announcing upcoming events and include name, date, time, and phone number to call for more information.

To determine how effective your marketing techniques are, ask the students at the beginning of each course how they heard about your class. But bear in mind they probably will only mention the last place they saw or heard about it. Some will surely mention the institution's catalog or brochure. This doesn't mean they didn't hear or see other promotions. It simply means that was the last place they looked before they signed up.

Planning the Class

Some community education departments require a detailed outline along with desired results the students should gain. Whether your department requests it or not, you should do this for your own use. It will provide you with the same guidelines and directions a road map does when you're planning a trip. It doesn't have to be lengthy or complicated. Just as you're flexible when taking an auto trip and may decide to take a side trip or cover more or less miles than planned, so it is with this plan. You will find, even with a class you've taught many times, different groups have varied needs and require diverse information.

Once you have your general outline, break it into segments and be specific about what you plan to start with and how long it will take. Allow the first few minutes of the first class to get acquainted, the length of time depends on the number of students and how much chatting takes place. Comment on information you receive and ask for clarification if you need to, and try to create a friendly atmosphere.

One-night classes are becoming more and more popular in community education departments and require instructors to make the point quickly and precisely. Whether you are doing a one-nighter or a longer class, you have to decide what sequence you will use, what materials you need to support your teaching, such as handouts, overheads, etc., what you hope your students will gain from each session, and the course, and how you will evaluate it.

Avoid dull information simply because you have it. One class entitled "How to Effectively Use Your Camcorder" attracted over thirty students but the instructor spent the first three-hour class explaining the history of the instrument and the complete workings of it. He lost at least ten students at the first break and another twelve didn't show up for any more classes. When he finally got around to actually shooting pictures with the camcorder in the fourth and final class, only six people remained. On the evaluations, all six suggested having him do a one-night class using the format of the last class.

Students usually don't care about the technical aspects of a camcorder or specifics about certain antiques or the history of Total Quality Management. As one student in a computer class said, "I don't want to build the darned thing. I just want to know how to use it!" Put yourself in the students' place and try to figure out what they want to know and how you can teach it to them. Don't beat yourself over the head if you feel you haven't done a good job or if evaluations are poor. Learn from your mistakes. Many a person who's been teaching the same subject for many years says, "I wish I could get in touch with the students I had the first couple of years and invite them back. Boy, have I learned a lot and could give them a lot more today."

Determine equipment you need such as an overhead projector, VCR, or other material and request it well in advance, preferably in writing so you have a record of the request. Find out requirements for handouts. How much in advance do you need to turn them in? Do you have to supply your own? Can you run them off on their equipment? When? A note on handouts. If you plan on handing out material, do so each session. If you hand everything out the first session, students may forget them so pass them out as you plan to use them.

Be over-prepared because you don't know how much material you will need until you actually teach the subject. Even when you've taught a subject again and again, you could run out of material with a class which doesn't need the basics and/or is a quiet group. Have several activities that relate to the topic and use them when needed. As you gain more experience, you'll pick up generic activities and ice breakers from other instructors, your reading, or even some of the your students.

SAMPLE COURSE OUTLINE

Sales Effectiveness Training

I. Introduction
    A. Assessment of students' needs
    B. Teacher's background and credentials
    C. Overview of course

II. Stages of the sales cycle
    A. Establishing relationship of trust
        1. Importance of making positive first impression
        2. Appropriate clothing for customer and product
            Using chameleon or mirroring approach
        3. Importance of nonverbals

    B. Mining expedition
        1. Fact gathering
        2. Importance of feelings in making decisions
        3. Verify what you think you heard

    C. Presentation
        1. Tie sales talk to the needs and feelings of buyer
        2. Stress benefits over features
        3. Pricing product or service
        4. Use of incentives
        5. Watch for clues so you don't oversell

    D. Assisting the buyer
        1. Most buyers need help to make right decision
        2. Don't sell something customer doesn't need

E. Closing the sale
      1. Buyers think why they shouldn't buy before they decide to buy
      2. 75% of all sales are made after fifth objection
      3. Assume the sale
      4. Use feel, felt, found approach
      5. Leave the door open and arrange for callback
   F. Servicing the sale
      1. Thank the customer and ask for feedback
      2. Thank the person who referred customer
      3. Follow up for materials and upgrades
   G. The cyclical nature of sales
      1. 80% of business comes from 20% of customers through repeats and referrals
      2. Importance of each stage of cycle
      3. Summation
III. Evaluations
   A. Ask students about impact of course information
   B. Hand out and collect written evaluations

If your class is several sessions, decide if you want to ask your students to do something before the next time you meet. Keep in mind people are busy; and if you ask them to do something that is time-consuming, they probably won't do it. If you ask them to complete an assignment or do a task, tell them you won't require them to bring an excuse from home if they don't do it. And live up to that promise.

Be flexible. Teaching adult education is great fun as you get to know each new class and try to give this group of individuals what you perceive to be their needs based on what they say and what you know.

You'll be teaching a subject you're thoroughly familiar with, but avoid trying to impart all your wisdom in one session, as much as you'd like to, unless it's a one-nighter. Go back over the description you created (with the help the community education staff) and read what you've told prospective students you'll teach them. Your task is to accomplish what you've promised.

THE INSTRUCTION

Who Teaches Non-credit Courses?

1. Credit classes are taught by people with academic credentials. Frequently these teachers have specialties because of additional research and/or studies. Non-credit courses may be taught by people with academic credentials, but not necessarily. Even if a person has degrees, one may want to teach something outside one's area of professional expertise. A lawyer may teach motorcycle repair. A metallurgist may teach science fiction writing. An elementary school teacher may teach French cooking. This doesn't mean any person who has an interest in a particular topic is qualified to teach a course. To teach a non-credit class, you must have proven expertise in the subject.

2. Whether or not non-credit teachers have college degrees, they do have a proven interest and knowledge in the subjects they're teaching. Students expect them to have practical information of the subject. A student in a silversmithing class said, "The instructor must have made every mistake in the book. She knows how to get out of any mess and fix everything."

3. Non-credit teachers may be professionally engaged in the subject they are teaching. This is not unusual and as a result, an increasing number of continuing education providers require instructors to sign statements pledging not to use class lists to promote their own businesses. Even if the institution where you're teaching doesn't require such a signed statement, ethics require instructors not to use classes to directly promote their businesses.

Most non-credit instructors teach because they want to share what they've learned. And most non-credit students are there because they want to be, not because it's required. This combination usually creates a positive experience for everyone.

The First Class

You planned your class. You've got your equipment, your handouts, and your students. Here you go. You're at least fifteen minutes early; you've picked up your class list and found your room. You're dressed appropriately. If you're offering a class on clay sculpting, a three-piece suit wouldn't be a logical choice. But neat, clean, and appropriate are the bywords on how to dress. Students expect their instructors to look and act professionally. Whether we like it or not, everybody discriminates by appearance and we never get a second chance to make a good first impression.

If you're not used to speaking in front of people, you're probably scared, or at least apprehensive. In spite of this, remember you know more about the subject you're going to teach than anyone else, so relax. Greet your students with a smile and friendly "hi" as they enter the room. This is not the time to be unloading your briefcase, you should have been early enough to have already done that. Ask them to identify themselves as they sit down so you can learn whether the person registered as Robert prefers to be called Bob, Rob, R. J., or Robert.

When class time arrives or all students are there, introduce yourself. Don't assume they remember your name from the class schedule. You've already established your expertise with the department to teach this class. Sometimes your credentials are included in class description, such as "Antique shop owner Jane Doe explains how and where to shop for antiques and collectibles." Even if this is the case, your first meeting with your new class should include a short autobiography defining your proficiency. Using the example above, Jane Doe might tell how she grew up in an area and home rich in early American history and began accumulating antiques from that period in her teens. She continued to build her collection over the years and eventually went to work for an auction house specializing in that period.

Twenty years ago, she converted a garage into her first antique shop. Now she owns her own building, a former century home, and has turned it into a premier shop. She might either invite students to drop in to the shop or make a field trip out of it. If she has written articles and given other workshops, she might include that information also.

Some instructors may be reluctant to stand in front of group of strangers and talk about themselves but doing so is helpful to the students. It lends credibility to the information the teacher will be providing. But even more important, it makes the teacher more human. An introduction should be the first item on your lesson plan. Teachers who find this difficult could hand out a short printed biography, which includes any information that involves their aptitude for this subject.

After the introduction, ask each student to state why (s)he signed up for this class. This is also the time to determine skill levels. Making notes of these remarks helps you keep them in mind. This exchange with the students helps them feel more at ease with you and the other students and opens up the possibility of feeling free to ask questions and offer opinions later and provides you with valuable information in teaching this particular group of students.

After the students introduce themselves and identify their needs, give your name again and outline the reasons you wanted to teach this class. If you are still apprehensive, be honest. Tell the students this is the first time you've taught, or maybe even spoken in public, and you're afraid of making a mistake. Ask them to help you by being supportive. You'll find they understand and are on your side. Fear of public speaking ranks number one with American adults. Death is number four. So the students can empathize. Make eye contact with the students as you're talking with them. If you're not used to public speaking, this takes practice. You might want to take a non-credit class on the subject and/or join a local Toastmasters chapter.

Unless your topic is a somber one, try to make it fun for your students (and yourself). You want to create enthusiasm and get them as excited about the subject as you are. If you're comfortable making puns or telling a few jokes, then do so, but keep them in good taste and don't make fun of anyone. And don't overdo the joke telling unless you're teaching a class in humor. Leave your stand-up routines for the local comedy club open mike night.

If you have a printed outline, pass it out at this point and go over it so your students know what the class will cover. If this is a short class, you probably won't have a printed outline. In that case, tell the class what you plan to cover and how. This is also the time to establish class rules and procedures. Explain when breaks will come; whether you want students to ask questions as you go along or write them down and ask at the end of the class; if and how they may make up a missed class; materials and equipment they'll need for future sessions; and other pertinent details.

You might explain how you plan to present the topic and encourage their questions and comments.

You may also wish to ask about their experience in this specific subject. We've outlined some of the general reasons people sign up for continuing education, but their experiences and backgrounds run the gamut from the person who knows nothing at all about the subject to one who has spent his or her life in that profession. Hopefully, you won't get that spread in the same class, but it can happen. When you encounter a professional or an expert in the class, hope you know at least as much as (s)he does. And don't hesitate to use the "expert" to add information when appropriate.

Classroom Techniques

The Lecture. This is the most used method of teaching for credit classes and may or may not be the best vehicle for non-credit. The lecture requires more preparation and skill than activities and/or demonstrations. You not only have to put it together but you need to rehearse. If this is the technique you plan to use make an outline and note important points and statistics, but don't read it, refer to your notes from time to time as you need to. There's nothing more boring than listening to a teacher drone on while students look at the top of the instructor's head. Some things to keep in mind if you're going to use this method are as follows:

1. You have to assess the students' background and experience so you can target the lecture to them. Since you probably won't have this information until the first class, you have to be flexible in your presentation.

2. Use anecdotes, concrete examples, and dramatic contrast to illustrate points. Make eye contact and use gestures to keep students' interest.

3. Some instructors move out from behind a desk or podium to make better contact with the students. Walk around if you want to, but not so much students get dizzy trying to follow you. (One instructor walked around so much that on his evaluation form a student suggested nailing the instructor's shoes to the floor to keep him in one place.)

4. Use questions to stimulate and motivate students. Above all, summarize at the conclusion of each major point. An effective summary in-

cludes repetition and reinforcement. Professional speakers know a presentation features a summary at the beginning and the end. The suggestion is, "Tell them what you're going to tell them. Tell them. Then tell them what you told them."

5. Be aware of your vocabulary. Your students come from every walk of life and level of education, so use simple words. People with experience in any field are used to jargon and idioms peculiar to that specialty. If you think your students might not understand a specific word or phrase, watch for confused expressions or better yet, explain as you are introducing an unfamiliar word or phrase. It's better to stop and define than to assume they understand what you're talking about because their lack of comprehension could prevent future comprehension.

Question/Answer. Proper use of questions is probably the most effective teaching mechanism. This is especially true for non-credit classes. The major reasons questions and answers are so effective is that students participate more fully than in the lecture technique. It also lets the instructor know how well (s)he is doing getting the subject across. Many teachers find they're covering material they don't need to include or need to expand on information they felt the students had grasped. Several points to remember in questioning:

1. Use specific questions which can't be answered yes or no. Don't ask the class in general for an answer; ask each student, if time permits. If the class is large and time is short, alternate the students you call on.

2. Avoid telling a student (s)he is wrong. Adults are sensitive and if criticized, they'll be reluctant to say anything in the future. In addition, their embarrassment prevents learning. This doesn't mean you endorse incorrect information. The instructor could say, "Perhaps I didn't ask the right question"; "Maybe I didn't cover that point clearly enough"; or "That's part of it. Can anyone add to that?"

3. Use questions to arouse curiosity, to assess the students' understanding, and which allow students to participate.

4. Call the students by name and ask open-ended questions such as "What do you think of that?" "How does that strike you?"

Discussion Groups. Discussions are a popular way to teach many subjects. People are used to this from their working environment, organizations, and other classes. Small groups of three to six work the best when the class is large enough and your subject lends itself to this technique. One of the reasons students take classes is to meet others and discussion groups help them get to know each other more quickly. Small groups facilitate sharing and understanding. Some points to remember in developing a discussion format:

1. There must be an objective or purpose for the discussion. Otherwise, it becomes simply a buzz session and aimless sharing of opinions.

2. A case study is an excellent vehicle for development of a meaningful discussion. A class in Customer Service might explore ways to deal with angry customers and ways to prevent problems before they start.

3. It may be a good idea to involve students in development of the discussion format, including planning the activities, monitoring the discussion, and presenting conclusions.

4. The groups should be told to select a recorder who will note conclusions and present them to the rest of the class.

5. A time limit should be established and a five-minute warning announced so each group can finish in the allotted time. Some instructors find it helpful to assign specific tasks to be finished the first five or ten minutes, the second five or ten minutes, and so forth, announcing the time so each group can move to the next task.

6. The instructor should walk around and listen in on each groups to make sure one or two students haven't taken over and stifled the opinions of others. This is probably the biggest trap to avoid when using this technique.

The Demonstration. Subjects such as wallpapering, quilting, and computer operation are learned more quickly and effectively using the demonstration technique. Some of the things to think about with this format are the following:

1. Each student needs the proper equipment. This can be accomplished by requiring each student to bring it, or by adding a materials fee to the course, so you or the department can supply it. For example, in the case of computer operations, you should have extra disks; scissors for quilting; or other equipment if students forgot to bring theirs.

2. One problem arises with classes where equipment is used. Using quilting as an example, do you send samples home with students so they can work on them until the next class? Or do you collect everybody's work and bring it back the next time? There's no right answer. If you collect everybody's work, you not only have to cart everything yourself, but you won't know whether the students have learned the subject without you to guide them. On the other hand, if they take them home, will they remember to bring the samples back?

3. We learn better by doing than by watching. Therefore watching an instructor measure and hang a length of wallpaper may not prepare students to do it themselves.

4. Don't assume you have all the answers. You may have learned to brush wallpaper paste on the back of the paper and assumed that's the only way to do it. When a student asks why you can't put the paste on the wall and hang the paper that way, you may be tempted to call that method impractical. Bite your tongue and admit you've never tried that way but it might work. By the way, this method is not only faster, it's easier to clean up. Many smart teachers have learned new methods and/or gained additional information from their students.

You'll sometimes find, even with a subject you've taught many times, you may cover more or less than you expect. When teaching a subject new to you, it's better to be over-prepared than under-prepared. This suggestion is made several times throughout this book and repeated because it's so important to remember. There's nothing more embarrassing than running out of material before running out of class time.

THE STUDENTS

Who Takes Your Classes?

Let's look at some of the reasons people sign up for non-credit classes:

1. To learn or enhance a skill for one's personal use and/or pleasure. This could include subjects like quilt-making, woodworking, improving your memory, time management, or publishing your own book. The list includes anything that involves a hobby or avocation.

2. To learn or improve one's skills for professional use. Subjects could include business law, how to start your own business, effective business

writing, and improving communication techniques. Memory-improvement, time management, stress management, and many other subjects could also fall into this category.

3. For social reasons. Many people want to expand their circle of friends. They may take classes in dancing, drama, or writing personal ads or any other type of class. A large percentage of students, particularly senior citizens, fall into this category but usually don't admit it. Sometimes they don't care what they learn as long as the class meets on Tuesdays, is one their friends like, or answers some other requirement.

4. Someone else enrolled them. Sometimes a daughter, mother, husband, or friend signed the student up for a class they thought the student would like and/or benefit from. This may turn out to be true or not.

Senior citizens make up a significant market for many community education departments and may be more drawn to day classes than night ones. There's no reason why the same class can't be offered on weekdays for seniors and evenings for the general population. If you're offering a daytime class, hoping to attract seniors, don't exclude younger students by labeling it a seniors class. It could be listed two places in a schedule, under a seniors category and in the general catalog.

Senior citizens are fun to teach and frequently are more liable to contribute than some other age groups. They've lived a long time and have acquired a lot of information during their lives. If they don't agree with something you've said, they'll say so. If they don't understand something, they'll ask. And if they're bored, they'll let you know. Teachers of seniors often say they come out of those classes learning more than they've taught.

Student Behaviors & Teaching Techniques

Teaching adults is different from teaching children since you're dealing with people your own age or older. As stated earlier, there's also a vast difference between teaching credit and non-credit classes and major differences why people sign up for them. Regardless of the subject you're teaching, you have to be a student of human nature as you deal with various types of students.

The Class Expert. This may be someone in the profession or someone who has studied it extensively. Since a good teaching technique for non-credit classes encourages students to ask questions and add information, you don't want to "put down" this student. If you do, it could discourage others from participating. You can use the expert to your advantage by asking if (s)he has anything to add. When doing this, you gain an ally, have someone else verify what you've said, and sometimes learn something you may not have known before. The problem comes when the "expert" contributes and questions everything you say. Try to be pleasant but firm, and inform him or her you can't possibly cover everything you want to cover with all the interruptions. Most of the time, this works. In extreme cases, a teacher may have to ignore the expert student and call on others. It's important to remember you are in charge of the class and it's your responsibility to teach a certain subject. Other students in the class will appreciate your taking care of this problem. Teachers who have problems with this concept might wish to take a non-credit class in assertiveness.

The Quiet Class. At the other end of the spectrum is the quiet class. The class which includes students who ask a lot of questions and/or express opinions and add information may make it difficult to cover all your material. But the quiet class puts the entire burden on you and you could run out of material before you run out of time. This is one reason why you should be over-prepared instead of risking being under-prepared.

When you start your class, you have already asked each student why (s)he signed up. You also have encouraged the students to ask questions and make statements during the class instead of waiting for breaks or the end of the class, saying "It's quite likely other students also want, or need, to know what you have to ask or say." This usually is sufficient, especially when you look at your students as you're teaching and pause occasionally, allowing time for student participation. If the class (and the topic) lends itself to small group discussions, brainstorming, and role playing, you might try that to loosen up the class.

Another method that works is to go around the class from time to time and ask each student "What have you found . . . ?" or "What do you think about this?" Avoid questions that can be answered yes or no, and don't just throw the question out to the class. If you do, no one may volunteer or you may get answers and opinions from one or two of the most extroverted students. It's important to establish a nonjudgmental attitude with the students; if you consistently challenge or argue with your students, you discourage participation. At the end of each session, you might want to ask your students (one at a time) what each plans to do as a result of the information gained in this session. This is not the same as assigning homework, since most people who take non-credit classes have no time (or desire) to do homework. The answers to this question help you plan where to start the next session and provide insight as to your effectiveness in communicating the subject.

Negative Students. There are two types of negative students, those who sit quietly and appear to sulk and those who are verbal and attack most things you say. The former type usually doesn't affect the class significantly since most times other students aren't aware of it. However, this type can significantly affect you as you try to win him or her over. Try to involve this student in a positive or success-oriented question/answer format. Through this, you may be able to assess the interests of the negative student and stimulate participation. This may not work. As anyone knows who has studied listening, our ability to communicate depends on the ability of someone else to listen. If attempts to involve the student in a positive way do not work, avoid looking at this student and make every effort to look at more attentive students.

The verbal negative student is different; everyone is aware of this student and can catch the negative influence if you don't control it. As with the class expert, you may have to ignore this student or even ask him or her to refrain from making comments if other attempts fail.

The Unruly Student. This type is fortunately rare in non-credit classes. This student may disagree with you and/or others and generally disrupt the class. Try all reasonable strategies such as trying to ignore the student and the behavior. Next politely ask for cooperation. If this fails, you might have to escort the student to the office or individual in charge. You can either give the other students something to do or schedule a break while you're gone. When you return to class, avoid making accusatory statements. Simply say, "Now where were we?" or something equally as neutral.

Considerations When Teaching Older Adults
by Carol Cohen

1. Be prepared. Older students often ask probing questions and you need to really know your subject. However, even when you do, someone may still come up with a question you can't answer. If this happens, admit it, don't pretend you do know. If appropriate, you might want to ask other students if they have the answer. It would be a good idea to research the question and bring the answer to the next session.

2. Have a lively and interesting teaching style. This is necessary particularly if your class is after lunch or in the evening. Otherwise you may find students snoozing if you drone on. Pay attention to the participants' responses to you, including their body language. If they seem bored, break into small discussion groups or use a visual aid.

3. Be aware of the physiological changes in older adults. Speak loudly and clearly and provide regular breaks if the class is longer than an hour. Provide easy-to-read handouts (when relevant) using light colored paper with information double spaced using 12-point or larger type.

4. Many students come to class looking for more than just learning the subject you're teaching. People often come to meet and interact with others, this is particularly true of senior citizens. Provide plenty of opportunities for students to get to know each other, including first session ice breakers, small discussion groups, and field trips.

5. Whenever possible, include class participation. Many older adults have had interesting life experiences that may contribute greatly to the course. This has the double advantage of enhancing your class and building the self esteem of the speaker. Some instructors have reservations about this because they fear the senior will take up too much time by going on and on. This is usually not the case, but if it does happen, it's your responsibility to gently tell the speaker you need to move on.

6. Retired people sometimes have more time than others, so provide information students can use outside of class. This may include recommended books, videos, or events happening in the community.

Evaluation

What if They Don't Come Back?

The man who taught the course on camcorders should have suspected something when the class dwindled from thirty down to six. But what do you do if your class of ten drops to eight the second week and six the third week? Sometimes you'll be lucky enough to have a student tell you they're not going to be able to come back, but most of the time, they simply don't show up. If you want to give out your phone number the first class and invite them to call you, it may work. But not necessarily. It is questionable whether it's a good idea for you to call absentees or not. If this is the first time you've taught this subject, you might want to discuss your concerns with the head of the department. But bear in mind, this problem happens to all instructors and many never really know why.

How Do You Know if They've Learned Anything?

At the end of the class, pass out evaluations if your department has provided them. It should be noted some evaluations are better than others and may or may not provide the information you wish they did. Pass out the evaluations and ask your students to simply put them on the desk or table nearest the door. This may help the students be more candid since they know you won't know who filled each one out. Read them and try to learn how to make your class as helpful to the students as possible. Also, try not to be depressed when you read something that doesn't have anything to do with your teaching.

Let's say your department either doesn't provide evaluation forms or you feel they don't provide the data you would like, how will you know the students have learned anything? The answer is you may not. If they've made a quilt square or learned how to write a letter on a computer and got it to print out, you know they got that far. But will they be able to do it without you? You may never know. Unlike credit classes, you don't give a final exam. If you planned on doing that, most of your students would probably go on break and not come back or simply stand up and walk out. There are no final grades given, although sometimes CEUs are earned to meet specific licensing or employment requirements. However, even then, usually the only requirement is that they attended the class.

As stated at the beginning, there's a big difference in teaching credit and non-credit classes. Non-credit teachers are usually more pragmatic. They know you can't teach many things as you would English, calculus, or engineering. Many non-credit subjects are more ethereal and less specific. Non-credit teachers can present the information in a nonjudgmental atmosphere and rely on students to have absorbed it. If students come back week after week or take more classes from you, you'll be pretty sure they're learning what they signed up for. Non-credit teachers are really facilitators. It will be the students' response to your teaching and whether they use it in their day-to-day life that is the real test. And you probably will never know it.

Occasionally, former students takes another class from you or accidentally bump into you and tells you how well that method of hanging wallpaper worked, how they've mastered the computer, or how they received a promotion at work using some of the techniques they learned in your course. Those are the bonuses. Teaching non-credit classes is a great way to share information and excite others about things you love. And you also meet some great people and may even make some new friends. What else would you like to teach?

Teacher's Self-evaluation Form

Class_____ Date_____

Instructions: Grade each of the following on a scale of 1-5 (5 being the highest) in terms of your perception of the teacher's behavior, characteristics, and effectiveness.

Classroom Evaluation

Preparation for class _____

Communication of classroom expectations _____

Command of subject matter _____

Professional and businesslike class behavior _____

Tests and evaluations reflect classroom lectures, discussions, and objectives _____

Encouragement of students participation _____

Course Related Factors

Utilization of supplemental teaching aids _____

Teacher Evaluation

Consideration for differing opinions _____

Consideration for individuals as persons _____

Sense of humor _____

Rating compared to other teachers _____

Personal appearance _____

Appropriateness of length of course _____

Verbal evaluation from students _____

Written evaluations from students _____

Retention of students _____

Teacher's greatest strengths _____

_____

Teacher's greatest weaknesses _____

_____

Ways to improve course _____

_____

Thanks to Carol Cohen, Coordinator Senior Adult Education for the Community Education Department at Lakeland Community College, Kirtland, Ohio, for her help in the development and preparation of this publication.

REFERENCES

Greive, Donald. *A Handbook for Adjunct and Part-Time Faculty and Teachers of Adults.* Cleveland :Box 40092, Info-Tec, Inc. 1995.

OTHER EDUCATIONAL PRODUCTS FROM INFO-TEC

☐ A Handbook for Adjunct/Part-Time Faculty and
   Teachers of Adults. (Rev. 1995) $10.95*

☐ Teaching in College —
   A Resource for College Teachers. (Rev. 1994) $24.95*

☐ Teaching Strategies and Techniques —
   for Adjunct Faculty. $4.95*

☐ Total Quality Education —
   Teaching Techniques for Technical Educators. $4.95*

☐ Cooperative Learning —
   A Classroom Guide. $4.95*

☐ Quick Tips for College Teaching —
   Bookmarks, Set of Three. $1.00*

* Quantity Prices Available
Phone (216) 333-3157
Fax (216) 933-9285